Steck-Vaugh

WORLD MYTHS

The Adventures of Cú Chulainn

Reviewer
Raymond E. Gleason
Department of English
Northwestern University

STECK-VAUGHN
C O M P A N Y
A Subsidiary of National Education Corporation

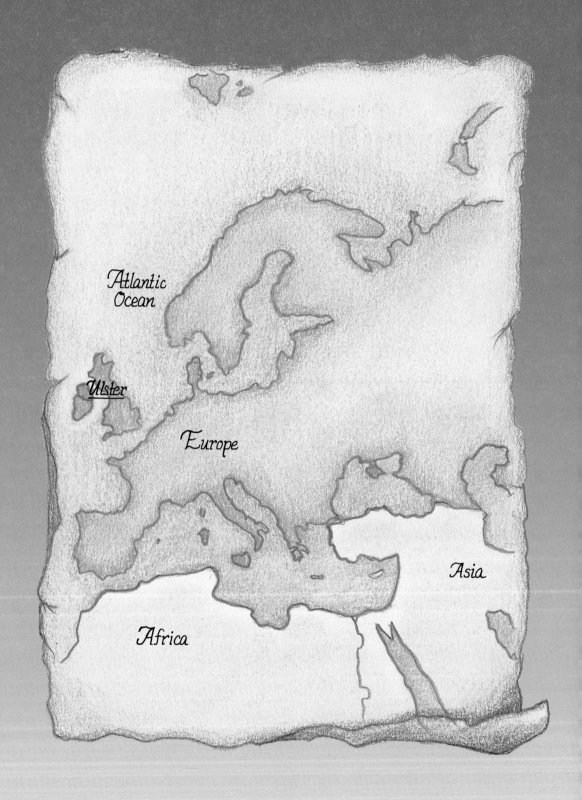

Atlantic
Ocean

Ulster

Europe

Asia

Africa

Introduction

The Uladh (ULL uh) people lived in northeastern Ireland over two thousand years ago. The name of the modern Irish province of Ulster comes from their name. These people produced a collection of myths called the Ulster Cycle, set in the kingdom of Ulster beginning around 100 B.C. The stories were passed down by word of mouth for more than eight hundred years before they were first recorded in writing. They were written in a language called Irish Gaelic (GAY lik). Gaelic uses the same alphabet as we do, but many of the letters stand for sounds that are different than they are in English.

The people described in the Ulster Cycle were brave warriors, and the greatest of their heroes was Cú Chulainn (koo KHUL in). Like many heroes worldwide, he was the son of a god. The Ulster Cycle tells about his life from his birth until his death at the age of twenty-seven. In the longest of the stories, "The Cattle Raid of Cooley," he defends the land of Ulster against the attack of a neighboring kingdom all by himself. Since the early Irish measured their wealth in cattle rather than in silver and gold, cattle raiding is a common theme in the stories.

The adventures of Cú Chulainn that follow take place when he is a little boy. In many myths throughout the world, heroes do not wait until they are grown up to display their powers and abilities. As you read, think about the powers Cú Chulainn displays and how the adults in the story react to him.

THE ADVENTURES OF CÚ CHULAINN

In ages long past, the very famous king Conchobar mac Nessa (KON koh var mak NES uh) ruled over the kingdom of Ulster, the greatest of the Irish kingdoms.

From his royal stronghold, Conchobar could look out over rolling hills laid out in a patchwork of golden fields of grain and green pastures dotted with fat cattle. Rivers brimming with fish ran among the hills. Great forests, filled with beast and fowl, grew all around. And beyond lay the sea, with its many treasures.

Adventure and mystery were common in Conchobar's court. One of his sisters, Dechtire (DEK ti ruh), had disappeared on her wedding day. The powerful god of the Otherworld had disguised himself as a mayfly and slipped into her drinking glass. She drank the mayfly and was transformed into a bird, as were fifty of her woman servants. They all flew away to the Otherworld.

Three years later,
they returned and changed back
into their human forms. Dechtire gave
birth to a baby son named Setanta (SHAY duhn duh).
Setanta was raised by his mother in a great oak house on the plains to
the south of the royal stronghold.

When Setanta was six, he heard about the shinty games at the
court of his uncle, the king. These games were played by one hundred
and fifty boys, who were divided into two teams. They used sticks to
knock a hard ball across the playing field into their opponents' goal.
The shinty playing field was the training ground for Conchobar's
warriors. As they played, they learned to fight and defend each other,
strengthening their spirits as well as their bodies.

Little Setanta begged his mother to let him go and play in the games. But she told him that he must wait until he was older. The boy was determined, however. He made a toy shield and spear for protection, took his shinty stick and ball, and set off by himself across the rough, winding road to the king's fortress.

Finally, he arrived and immediately spotted a group of young boys playing shinty. In his excitement, he ran onto the field to join them.

Shinty was a rough game. If a boy wished to play, he was expected to ask for protection from the other players. But Setanta did not know this.

The shinty players saw the unknown little boy running toward them and yelled out a warning. But Setanta paid no attention, so the boys seized their spears and flung all one hundred and fifty at him.

Setanta was as strong and quick as boys twice his age. He held out his toy shield and stopped all of the spears. The players then threw their shinty sticks and balls at him, but he easily dodged them all.

The little boy did not understand why he was being attacked. He became so enraged that his hair stood on end and crackled like fire. One of his eyes narrowed to an angry slit, and the other swelled and glared with fury. His mouth opened wide in a terrible snarl. Then he rushed at the frightened boys and tackled fifty of them before they could even turn to run.

The cries of the boys were heard by Conchobar, who came running out to see what was happening. He saw what seemed to be a small monster standing next to the pile of shinty players. He was shocked. "You have done much damage. Why have you treated these boys so roughly?" he asked Setanta.

"I only came to play with them. They tried to drive
me away as though I came to steal cattle," Setanta replied.

"You should know that you must ask for protection from the
shinty players. Who are you?" the king demanded.

"I am Setanta, your nephew, son of your sister, Dechtire," the little
boy answered. "I did not know I should have asked for protection
before playing."

Conchobar was surprised and pleased to see his nephew, who
looked himself again now that he had calmed down. Conchobar
arranged for Setanta to stay on at the court, and Setanta made peace
with the other boys. Over the next few weeks, he became an expert at
shinty and began to learn the techniques of a warrior.

One day, Culann (KULL in) the Blacksmith invited the king and about fifty warriors to his home for food and entertainment. That afternoon, as Conchobar and the warriors set out, they passed the shinty playing field. As usual, Setanta was beating all one hundred and fifty boys single-handed.

Conchobar stopped, called the boy over, and invited him to come along to Culann's feast. Setanta asked to finish his shinty game first. He said he would come to Culann's when the game was over. So he returned to his game, while Conchobar and the warriors rode over the hills in their chariots to Culann's home.

As the king and his men sat down at the feast, Culann asked Conchobar whether anyone else was expected. The king forgot all about Setanta and replied that everyone had arrived.

"Very well. I will order the servants to close the gates and unleash my hound. I have a fierce dog who guards my cattle and household. It takes three iron chains to hold him," Culann said with pride.

Some time later, Setanta approached Culann's gates, hitting the shinty ball with his stick as he walked. He paid no attention to the growling dog at the gate. As Setanta came closer, the dog began to bark loudly.

Inside Culann's house, Conchobar and those at the feast heard the wild barking of the hound. The king jumped to his feet, suddenly remembering his nephew. Everyone ran outside expecting to see the worst. Instead, they saw Setanta skipping through the gate. The huge dog lay dead on the ground, with a shinty ball in its throat. The warriors cheered the boy. Conchobar hugged him, glad that Setanta was safe.

But Culann hung his head sadly. "Of course, I am happy that you are all right, young lad," he said to Setanta. "But you have killed my best friend. That dog kept my land and property safe. Now I am at the mercy of thieves and villains."

Setanta thought for a moment. Then he asked Culann if the dog had a pup. When Culann told him that there was a pup, Setanta volunteered to take charge of training it.

"And until the pup is grown, I will be your hound," Setanta said. "I will guard the land all around. No one will dare even to look in the direction of your cattle or sheep while I am on guard."

Cathbad (KATH vuh), a druid leader of the Celtic people and father of the king, was attending the feast. He turned to his grandson and smiled. "From now on, Setanta, you will be called Cú Chulainn (koo KHUL in), Hound of Culann," he said. Everyone laughed. And so Setanta was forever after known as Cú Chulainn.

Not long after, Cathbad was teaching at the court. He had about one hundred students seeking to learn the secrets of the druids. On this day, one student asked Cathbad to tell the omen for the day.

"The warrior who takes up weapons for the first time on this day will have glory forever," Cathbad answered.

Cú Chulainn listened to this message. Then he ran off to his uncle, the king. "Cathbad has said that I must have weapons today," he cried, jumping up and down with excitement.

Conchobar was surprised. But he did not wish to go against the word of his father, so he gave the little boy a spear and a shield. Cú Chulainn was even stronger than when he had first come to Conchobar's court. Every weapon he was given bent and broke in his grasp. The only weapons that Cú Chulainn did not destroy were those belonging to Conchobar himself.

The little boy was holding these weapons when Cathbad came along and saw him. "How sad that such a young boy should be carrying weapons already," he remarked.

"But did you not tell him to do so?" Conchobar asked in surprise.

"I did not," Cathbad replied.

Conchobar turned to his nephew with anger and disappointment. "Hound! You have lied to me!" he said.

"Oh, no, dear uncle. I am only fulfilling the words I heard from Cathbad," the boy said.

Cathbad admitted that the omen must relate to Cú Chulainn, who was clearly destined to be a great warrior. Conchobar decided it was time to test the warrior skills of his nephew.

A chariot was ordered for Cú Chulainn, but it crumbled under his mighty force. As with the weapons, only the king's chariot was strong enough. The king's own chariot driver, Ibar (EE var), was called to travel with Cú Chulainn. Together, they set off to the borders of the kingdom of Ulster.

When they arrived at the border, Cú Chulainn dismissed the warrior on guard, Conall Cearnach (KO nuhl KYAR nuhk). Conall took one look at the little boy and laughed.

"You could guard the sheep and the poets, my boy. But a warrior would toss you into the sea with a pass of his hand," Conall said.

Cú Chulainn glared at Conall. Then he reached out and smashed his chariot. Conall had to walk all the way back home. And he never mocked Cú Chulainn again.

The boy then asked Ibar to take him to the highest point along the border. From the top of a rocky cliff, Cú Chulainn surveyed the countryside below. He could see all the fortresses along the border. He noted the lay of the land. He discovered the hiding places and the shallow areas where the streams could be crossed.

After studying all this, he ordered Ibar to take him to a fortress that belonged to three brothers who were enemies of Ulster. Their father had been killed by one of Conchobar's warriors. Since that time, they had taken revenge on many of Ulster's men.

Ibar was worried about Cú Chulainn, even though he was the strongest boy anyone had ever known.

"Why must you go in search of danger?" Ibar asked him.

"Why should I avoid it?" answered little Cú Chulainn.

Ibar said no more, and did as the boy requested. On their way to the fortress, they stopped to get a drink from a cool stream and rest in the shade, out of the hot afternoon sun. Cú Chulainn had just dozed off, when the three brothers rode up on their horses. They had their weapons drawn and ready. "Who are you and what do you want on our land?" they demanded.

"I am just a chariot driver," Ibar replied, then pointed to the sleeping Cú Chulainn. "And he is only a boy who has taken up arms just today. We are only passing by."

"We are not just passing by, and I am not just a boy," Cú Chulainn announced, rising to face the three brothers. "I am the Hound of Cúlann, and I have come to fight and avenge the deaths of Ulster's warriors."

The brothers grinned, thinking that it would be easy to kill the little boy. But they found that the Hound was as powerful a warrior as any they had ever met. Before the sun went down, Cú Chulainn had won the battle against all three brothers.

On the return journey, Cú Chulainn proved that he had power over animals as well as men. He saw deer grazing in the clearings at the edge of the forests. "I must trap a deer and bring it home alive for my uncle," he said.

He leaped from the chariot and ran toward the deer, which turned and fled. But Cú Chulainn ran swiftly alongside the finest one in the herd. When he passed it, he turned and stopped it, using only the look in his eyes. Then he led the deer back to Ibar and the waiting chariot. He tied the deer behind the chariot.

On they went. Cú Chulainn was becoming more and more excited as he thought about the battles he would fight as a mighty warrior.

Overhead, Cú Chulainn heard the honking of a flock of swans. A moment later, he had brought down twenty of the great white birds with his slingshot. The birds were only stunned. Cú Chulainn tied two of them to the sides of the chariot so that they flew along on either side.

Cú Chulainn was so excited, that the change he had experienced that first day on the shinty field came over him again. His hair stood up, crackling. His eyes changed. He looked as if he was going to battle.

As the chariot came over the last hill on the road to Conchobar's royal stronghold, the poet Leborcham (E vor kohm) looked out from the fortress. "A mad warrior is about to attack!" she cried. "His hair blazes like a fiery halo all about his head, and his face is twisted with rage! An immense deer runs behind, and two swans fly on either side of his racing chariot!"

Conchobar recognized the description of his nephew in his battle frenzy. He calmed the fears of the court. Then he ordered his strongest warriors to meet Cú Chulainn and quiet his rage.

When the chariot neared the
fortress, the warriors rode out and seized the
Hound. They plunged him into three vats of icy water to calm him.
Finally he returned to his normal state. Then he was given a white
linen tunic trimmed with gold and a green cloak fastened with a silver
pin. He dressed and looked like himself again. He was still only seven
years old.

Conchobar hugged the boy and stroked his shining hair. As they walked out to see the deer and the swans, the king said, "I am proud of you, my boy. And the Uladh will be proud to call you their hero. As Cathbad has said, you will live forever in the history of your people, Hound of Cúlann."

Glossary

avenge *v.* To get revenge for; get even.   p. 12

druid *adj.* Of a certain group of leaders of an ancient religion.   p. 9

enraged *adj.* Extremely angry; furious.   p. 6

lay of the land *n.* The way things are, such as certain features of the land.   p. 11

omen *n.* A sign of what is going to happen.   p. 9

Otherworld *n.* In some myths, a magical world separate from the real world.   p. 4

single-handed *adj.* All alone, without help from anyone.   p. 8

stronghold *n.* A strong, safe place like a fort.   p. 4

tunic *n.* An article of clothing, something like a long shirt, that reaches to the knees or below.   p. 14

vat *n.* A large tank or container for liquids.   p. 14

worldwide *adj.* Spread throughout the whole world.   p. 3

Acknowledgments

Steck-Vaughn Company

Executive Editor Diane Sharpe
Senior Editor Martin S. Saiewitz
Assistant Art Director Cynthia Ellis

Proof Positive/Farrowlyne Associates, Inc.

Program Development, Design, and Production

Illustration

Marcy Ramsey